BASICS OF HUMAN RESOURCE MANAGEMENT

SANJAY GOYAL DR. MUKTA GOYAL

Contents

Preface

To achieve the strategic aims and objectives of the employer, human resource management (HRM) is an activity carried out in businesses. More specifically, HRM concentrates on managing employees within businesses, with a focus on processes and procedures.

The corporate world is quickly realising the significance of human resource (HR) as an incomparable strength for achieving sustainable advantage due to the ever-escalating demands of the business environment. Nearly all B-schools and colleges that provide management courses give papers on the subject of HRM. However, the lack of literature on HRM makes it difficult for teachers and students to find pertinent and contextual information on the topic.

We hope that as you read this book, the students will concur that the topic of human resource management is fascinating. We provide a variety of examples from actual businesses to help ideas and concepts come to life and show how good human resource management is assisting businesses in succeeding. Each chapter demonstrates how a company can boost productivity by streamlining the procedures it uses to find and retain great talent. Additionally, we directly connect human resource management approaches to competitive tactics. This connection is important because it illustrates how a business might employ its people resources.

Sanjay Goyal
Dr. Mukta Goyal

ONE

Human Resource Management: Human Resource Planning/ Professional Job Designing, Job Analysis & Demand and Supply.

Introduction

What is HRM?

Human resource management, or HRM, is the process of managing personnel in a business, and it might include hiring, firing, training, and motivating them.

The process of hiring and developing individuals to increase their value to the company.

Human resource management is the organisational function in charge of all concerns concerning an organization's people. Compensation, recruitment, and hiring, as well as performance management, organisation development, safety, wellness, benefits, employee engagement, communication, policy administration, and training, are all examples of this.

Human resource management is a deliberate and all-encompassing approach to managing people, as well as the culture and environment of the workplace. It allows employees to contribute effectively and productively to the overall corporate direction as well as the achievement of the organization's goals and objectives when done correctly.

Members of the department supply the required information, tools, training, administrative services, coaching, legal and management counsel, and talent management oversight that the rest of the business requires to run smoothly.

Nature of HRM

Human resource management seeks to achieve each individual's as well as the organization's overall goals.

Nature of HRM are:

1. Pervasive Force

Human Resource Management is a necessary component of any business. It is widespread in nature and may be found at all levels of management in all businesses. Each manager is responsible for selecting the best applicant for the job and monitoring the development and happiness of each subordinate.

2. People Oriented

Human Resource Management is concerned with and appreciates people at work, both individually and collectively. It motivates employees to reach their maximum potential and, in turn, contribute their all to the company.

3. Action-Oriented

Human Resource Management adheres to rules, records, and policies, but it places a premium on action. The emphasis is on providing employees with an efficient and fast solution to any problems, tensions, or controversies they may be experiencing.

5. Future-Oriented

Organizations use long-term strategic planning to stay afloat and thrive in this competitive climate. Human resource management that is effective prepares individuals for present and future problems, which is especially important while working in an environment that is defined by rapid change.

6. Development Oriented

HRM is always working to improve employee development. To help employees attain their full potential, a variety of tools are used. Employees participate in training programmes to improve their skills and expertise. Employees are motivated through monetary and non-monetary incentives.

7. Enhance Employee Relations

HRM aids in the development of positive relationships among employees at all levels. It promotes mentoring and counselling to assist employees in difficult situations. Its goal is to foster a learning and growth-oriented culture within the company.

8. Interdisciplinary Function

It is interdisciplinary knowledge that has influenced Human Resource Management. Education, system theory, economics, psychology, and organisational behaviour are the five key fields of knowledge that it drives.

Scope of HRM

Human resource management encompasses a wide range of functions; every department and operation inside a business need human resources, even if it is simply operating machines.

Human resource management can be classified into three categories:

- HRM in Personnel Management
- HRM in Employee Welfare
- HRM in Industrial Relations

1.HRM in Personnel Management

The goal is to ensure that each employee's individual success contributes to the organization's overall growth in an indirect way.

2.HRM in Employee Welfare

This part of HRM is focused on the working environment and workplace facilities. It improves the working environment by removing workplace risks, ensuring job safety, and providing medical and health services, among other things.

3.HRM in Industrial Relations

The fundamental goal of this component is to keep the organisation in peace and harmony. It necessitates good communication with labour or employee unions, as well as carefully addressing their issues and resolving their conflicts.

Evolution of HRM?

Because of the connection of the difficulties in both domains, HRM, as a part of management discipline, has followed the pattern of management development.

Human Resource Management (HRM) is a relatively new word used to describe how an organisation manages its human resources. HRM is still growing into a mash-up of organisational behaviour, personnel management, labour relations, and labour law.

From the industrial revolution era to the present era, various stages to the development of management of human resource practices may be classified as follows:

1. Industrial revolution era— 19th century
2. Trade union movement era — close to the 19th century
3. Social responsibility era — beginning of the 20th century
4. Scientific management era— 1900-1920s
5. Human relations era— 1930s-1950s
6. Behavioural science era— 1950s-1960s
7. Systems and contingency approach era – 1960 onwards
8. Human resource management era — 1980 onwards

What are the challenges of HRM?

HRM challenges are critical functions in any firm. It is the process of managing people in order to improve their performance. Environmental, organisational, and individual problems, for example, are all possible HR challenges. Always keep in mind that these obstacles aren't about a single dimension; rather, they're about multi-dimensional concerns that need to be addressed right now.

In today's competitive world, the following are the major categories of Human Resource Management challenges.

Challenges Of HRM

1. Environmental Challenges
2. Organizational Challenges
3. Individual Challenges

Environmental Challenges

Environmental problems are external elements that exist in an organization's outer environment and can have an impact on the organization's management performance. External forces are nearly beyond the control of the organization's management.

These can be viewed as dangers to management and should be addressed immediately. The following is a list of human resource management issues that are also environmental challenges.

1. Rapid Change
2. Workforce Diversity
3. Globalization
4. Legislation
5. Technology
6. Job and Family Roles
7. Lack of Skills

Organizational Challenges

The elements that are found within the organisation are the sources of organisational problems for HRM. Although these issues arose as a result of environmental challenges, they can be managed to a large part by the organization's management.

Proactive HR managers recognise such obstacles ahead of time and take corrective action before they become severe problems. Competitive position and flexibility, organisational restructuring and downsizing concerns, the exercise of self-managed teams, the development of a suitable organisational culture, and other human resource management challenges face the business.

When an organization's labour is successfully utilised in conjunction with other variables of production, the environment's opportunities are realised and risks are removed. HR policies can have an impact on the organization's competitive position in the following ways.

1. Controlling Costs
2. Improving Quality
3. Developing Distinctive Capabilities
4. Restructuring

Individual Challenges

Individual decisions affecting unique employees are contained in the HRM's individual challenges. The manner in which employees are handled within organisations has an impact on organisational challenges. The following are the issues at the individual level.

1. Productivity
2. Empowerment
3. Brain Drain

4. Ethics and social responsibility
5. Job insecurity
6. Matching people and organization

What is meant to be an HR professional?

Human resources specialists play a critical role in the corporate world, and any company would benefit immensely from having one on staff. HR experts are responsible for not only dealing with business, strategy, planning, and development, but also for resolving conflicts and promoting company values.

The role of an HR professional

- **Promoting change within a business**- An HR professional should be able to examine a company's strengths and shortcomings and devise methods for developing certain competencies while utilising dormant skills within the organisation.
- **Hiring new staff members**- HR experts are frequently involved in the hiring of new employees, ensuring that they satisfy the required qualifications and are a suitable match for the company's culture.
- **Employee advocate**- Listening to employee concerns, understanding their viewpoint, and serving as a bridge between management and employees. HR practitioners should be able to deal delicately with employee difficulties.
- **Promoting workplace values**- When many diverse sorts of people work together, it's critical that they have common workplace values in order to achieve a common goal and avoid conflicts as much as possible. An HR professional's role is to promote the company's values.
- **Skill development**- In order to secure the firm's future, HR experts must focus on growing employees' talents in order to ensure that they will remain relevant inside the company in the long run.
- **Finding solutions to problems**- HR specialists, as functional experts, aid in identifying structural challenges inside a company and developing unique and effective solutions using their knowledge, skills, and background.
- **Strategic partner**- HR experts collaborate closely with management in developing plans to achieve objectives and advising leaders on what needs to be done to attain these objectives.

- **HR Leadership**- HR experts who lead HR teams are known as HR leaders. Their responsibilities and management responsibilities are similar, but they are believed to be exaggerated in terms of responsibility and management.
- **Change in regulations**- HR experts are frequently significantly involved in the implementation of new workplace legislation and contracts since they have value to provide in terms of employee advocacy and company advantages.
- **Handling disputes**- Workplace conflicts are unfortunately all too common. The role of the HR professional in a company is often to handle disagreements and act as a mediator.

The qualities of a good HR professional

When it comes to working in the subject of human resources, certain personal qualities and talents are extremely beneficial. Just because a person doesn't have certain talents at birth doesn't mean they can't learn them over time.

- **Flexibility**- Flexibility is a critical characteristic of every HR practitioner. They'll almost certainly have to manage many activities and projects at once, as well as be able to swiftly determine where they'd be most beneficial at any given time.
- **Good listener**- Being a human resources practitioner necessitates a great deal of listening. Listening to employee concerns as well as boss criticism It's critical to be a good listener and avoid zoning out during crucial conversations.
- **Confidence**- HR specialists will occasionally be called upon to give talks regarding new workplace regulations to big groups of employees. Confidence not only makes their professions easier, but it also makes them more pleasurable.
- **Caring heart**- Having an HR expert with a loving heart is absolutely beneficial to employees. This means that when it comes to complaints, new regulations, and so on, the needs of the employees will be carefully acknowledged.
- **Communication**- As an HR professional, clear communication is critical because you frequently operate as a go-between for several parties, and you don't want to end up with a game of broken telephone on your hands.

- **Management**- While HR professionals are not managers, many of their responsibilities are similar to those of managers, and they collaborate closely with the management team.
- **Organisational skills**- As an HR professional, having organisational skills will come in handy. Because HR professionals are always required to create new structures and plans, organisational skills assist them in putting these plans together in a cohesive and effective manner.

Global perspectives of HRM?

- **Societal objective.** To be socially responsible in response to societal needs and issues while limiting the negative impact on the organisation. Organizations that fail to use their resources for the greater good of society may face constraints. For example, society may enact legislation that restricts the use of human resources.
- **Functional objective.** Maintain the department's contribution at a level that meets the needs of the organisation. When Human Resource Management is more or less complex than the organisation requires, resources are wasted. The degree of service provided by a department must be appropriate for the organisation it serves.
- **Organizational objective.** Recognize that human resource management exists to help organisations function more effectively. HRM is not a goal in and of itself; it is merely a tool to help the business achieve its fundamental goals. Simply said, the department's purpose is to help the rest of the company.

Demand and supply
Demand Forecasting:
Human resource planning includes a quantitative component called demand forecasting. It is the process of estimating the organization's future human resource needs of all types and sizes.

- **Factors:**

Forecasting of demand for human resources depends on certain factors such as:

1. The organization's employment trend must be examined for at least the last five years in order to determine future needs.
2. Due to retirement, death, resignation, termination, and other factors, the organisation must determine its replacement needs.
3. Another factor is an increase in production. Better employees with abilities and potential are required to increase production. Productivity leads to growth, but it is contingent on market demand for the company's goods. Demand for skilled workers may increase as a result of the increased demand.

Organizational growth necessitates the hiring of more skilled workers. The annual budget seres as the foundation for human resource forecasting. The budget determines the manufacturing strategy. As manufacturing grows, so does the need for more people with certain talents and technology.

1. ***Methods of Demand Forecasting:***
2. Executive Judgment
3. Work Load Forecasting
4. Statistical Techniques

Supply Forecasting:

Supply forecasting is the process of estimating human resource supply based on an examination of present human resource inventory and future availability.

Sources of Supply:

Internal and external sources are used to estimate the supply of human resources.

· **Internal Factors:**

The output from established training programmes for employees and management development programmes for executives, as well as the organization's existing reservoirs of skills, potentials, and creative capacities, are all sources of internal human resource supply.

· **External Factors:**

Local and national variables are two types of external forces.

(a) Local Factors:

1. Densities of the population within the enterprise's reach.
2. Other employers' current and prospective wage and salary structures.
3. The unemployment rate in the area.
4. Employees who are available on a part-time, temporary, or casual basis.
5. The output of government and private-sector-run educational and training institutions in the local area.
6. Local transportation and communication services are available.
7. Availability of residential facilities, etc.

(b) National Factors:

1. Trends in growth of working population of the country.
2. National demands for certain categories of human resources such as technical and management professionals, computer professionals, medical practitioners, technicians, secretaries, craftsmen, graduates etc.
3. The output from universities, technical and professional institutions.
4. Impact of changes in educational patterns.
5. Cultural patterns, social norms and customs.
6. Impact of government training schemes.
7. Impact of government policies in respect of employment regulations.
8. Migration and immigration patterns.
9. Impact of national educational facilities.

What is Job Design?

Outlining the task, duties, responsibilities, qualifications, procedures, and relationships required to complete the specified set of tasks is referred to as job design. In other words, job design incorporates the task components as well as the pattern of employee interaction, with the goal of meeting both the organisational and social demands of the jobholder.

The goal of a job design is to organise the work in such a way that it reduces employee boredom and dissatisfaction caused by the repetitive nature of the labour.

- **When it comes to work design, the management employs a number of significant tactics and procedures. These are the following:**

A. **Job Rotation**

Employment rotation is a lateral change in the job role or position, which occurs between job levels and is not to be confused with a promotion. Because it limits a person's ability to advance in his or her work. It is done on a temporary basis, with personnel returning to their prior position after a set period of time.

It has numerous advantages, including: -

- Learning
- **Flexibility**
- **Employee replacement**

B. **Job Enlargement**

As the term implies, job enlargement entails the addition of additional tasks or activities to an employee's current employment. This means that employees will engage in a variety of activities on the workplace, which will alleviate boredom and reduce boring work. **Job expansion has a number of advantages for both the person and the company are: -**

- Earn a higher wage
- Give more autonomy
- Career growth

C. Job Enrichment

This strategy involves incorporating the motivators into an existing work. Adding skill variety, extra tasks, providing feedback, giving the job significance, and boosting autonomy are just a few examples. The employee's job becomes more meaningful as a result of this strategy.

If you're not sure what the difference is between job enlargement and job enrichment, here's what you need to know: - Job enlargement makes the employment more motivating by increasing the scope of the employee's job, whereas job enrichment involves adding motivators to the employee's current job.

The following are some of the advantages of job enrichment:

- Increase satisfaction

○ Better psychological states

D. Job Simplification

It is the process of removing a few tasks from a work to make it more focused on the core task. The goal of this strategy is to implement better work practises that will increase output while lowering expenses and costs.

○ **Obviating unnecessary work**
○ **Make employee more focused**

While designing the job, the following aspects are to be taken into the consideration:

- The most important need for a job design is to precisely outline the work that an employee is expected to complete. A task is a piece of labour that is allocated to an individual and must be completed within a certain amount of time.
- Management must determine the level of incentive that must be imposed on an employee in order for the work to be accomplished successfully. As a result, managers must create occupations that motivate their people.
- Managers must make a vital decision about how many resources are needed to complete a specific task. As a result, efforts should be made to make the best use of organisational resources while planning the work so that the organisation does not face any difficulties owing to a lack of resources.
- When jobs are allocated to an individual, he decides to do them because of the benefits that come with them. As a result, the management must integrate compensation, bonuses, incentives, benefits, and other remuneration methods for the employees in the job design.

As a result, the job should be developed with the goal of finding a match between the job and its performer, so that the job is completed effectively and the performer is satisfied while executing it and gives it his all.

Factors affecting Human Resource Planning.
What Is Human Resource Planning?

- · Human resources in an organisation are more than just the workforce; they are the sum of an organization's knowledge, skills, aptitude, creative abilities, and talents, as well as the values, attitudes, and benefits that each individual brings to the company.

- Human resource planning is a systematic and planned method for assessing an organization's existing human resource situation and forecasting future labour requirements. Human resource planning, also known as workforce planning, assists organisations in recruiting, retaining, and optimising the deployment of people they need to accomplish strategic business objectives and respond to market and general environment changes.

- Projecting future labour requirements and establishing methods for deploying this talent to avoid skills shortages or surpluses is an important aspect of human resource planning. The goal is to develop a skill balance that is based on the company's demands and goals. As a result, HR planning must be a continuous process with a framework and monitoring system that allows the organisation to provide enough lead time for personnel recruitment and training to meet future expectations.

Why Is Human Resource Planning Important?

Human resource planning enables businesses to meet their current and future talent demands by allowing human resource managers to anticipate and develop the skills that are most valuable to an organisation, as well as providing the company with the best staffing mix in terms of available skill sets and personnel numbers. Proper planning also paves the way for future growth by building a talent pool capable of filling leadership positions. Human resource planning also helps integrate human capital management with business strategy in the long run.

Factors Affecting Human Resource Planning

Human Resource Planning is influenced by a number of things. Human resource planning is the process of organising an organization's human resources. HRP forecasts the organization's future human resource requirements and plans appropriately. As a result, there are a variety of elements that influence Human Resource Planning in this process.

Let's talk about the aspects that influence human resource planning: -

v. **Organizational Growth Cycle and Planning:**

Each organisation will be in a different stage of its life cycle. Existence, survival, maturity, renewal, and decline are the five stages of an organization's growth cycle. HRP's success is also determined by the stage of the growth cycle in which the company is now operating. As a result, the Human Resource department must understand and take into account the organization's growth cycle stage while designing the Human Resource planning process.

v. **Environmental uncertainties:**

Certain factors, such as the labour market, the nation's economic development, natural disasters, and government policies, are beyond the management's control. These factors will have an impact on any company's HRP.

v. **Outsourcing:**

Many organisations are outsourcing many tasks these days in order to save money, time, effort, or all three. Security, canteen, office assistance, system supporters, maintenance staff, and other services are commonly outsourced. When the HRP is completed several times, there may be less indicators concerning the organization's future outsourcing plan. Hence this will also affect the HRP.

v. **Nature of Jobs being filled**

HRP's success is also determined by the nature of the positions being filled. From job to job, demand and supply, alternative employees, and turnover ratios differ. Each post takes a varied amount of time to fill. All of this is important and has an impact on human resource planning.

v. **Type & Quality of Forecasting Information:**

HRP is based on the future forecasting of the organization's people requirements, as mentioned earlier. The information needed to calculate the manpower required is gathered in a variety of methods. The quality and reliability of the information obtained is determined by the type of data used and the technique employed to acquire it.

It's also worth noting that the sort of data to gather and the way to collect it must be determined based on the nature of the job to be filled, the organization's life cycle, previous experiences, and so on. This is one of the most crucial things that will directly affect HRP.

v. **Time Horizons:**

Many things are included in the time horizon, such as how many years you are projecting, how many years HRP is planned for, how many years data you are using, and how far ahead you are anticipating the Human resource requirement. As a result, the organisation must aim for a precise time frame that is neither too long nor too short. Data should not be more than a few years old. You should not plan too far ahead of time or too late. Time horizons must be given a lot of attention because they are one of the decisive variables.

v. **Type & Strategy of organization:**

Depending on the market, products, competitors, government legislation, and other factors, the organisation may need to adjust its strategy. In some circumstances, the HRP will be influenced by the organization's kind and strategy. As a result, before embarking on manpower planning, the HR department must analyse all options.

What is job analysis?

Definition:

Job analysis refers to a systematic process of collecting all information about a specific job, including skill requirements, roles, responsibilities and processes in order to create a valid job description.

Job analysis also gives an overview of the physical, emotional & related human qualities required to execute the job successfully.

Importance of job analysis

Job analysis is a crucial stage in ensuring the best applicant is chosen.

The employer can use job analysis to help with recruitment and selection, performance management, remuneration and benefits, and so on. It allows employees to have a clear understanding of what is expected of them.

Methods of job analysis

◦ Interviews

One technique to generate an appropriate work description is to ask an employee for details about their job. Employers will inquire about specific tasks as well as a breakdown of the responsibilities of those in a given job.

◦ Observations

An employer may also opt to observe employees as they perform their jobs, noting the tasks they complete and the abilities required to complete them. Observations are effective for processes involving physical tasks and product outcomes.

◦ Surveys

Surveys are used to determine how frequently a task is accomplished or how frequently a skill set is used. These surveys can take the form of highly structured questionnaires in which employees respond to questions about their jobs using a scale. Employees can also use surveys to answer open-ended questions more casually.

◦ Work logs

Employers can ask for a written account of daily labour for a specific time period. This enables an employee to provide a detailed explanation of their job's regular responsibilities as well as the timeframes required for each task.

Advantages of Job Analysis

◦ Provides First Hand Job-Related Information
◦ Helps in Creating Right Jb-Employee Fit
◦ Helps in Establishing Effective Hiring Practices
◦ Guides through Performance Evaluation and Appraisal Processes
◦ Helps in Analyzing Training & Development Needs
◦ Helps in Deciding Compensation Package for a Specific Job

Disadvantages of Job Analysis

- Time Consuming
- Involves Personal Biasness
- The source of Data is Extremely Small
- Involves Lots of Human Efforts
- Jb Analyst May Not Possess Appropriate Skills
- Mental Abilities Can't be Directly Observed

TWO

RECRUITMENT: PROCESS, SOURCES, METHODS, TRAINING AND DEVELOPMENT

Introduction

Recruitment and its process

Recruitment is a core function of the Human Resource department. It is a process that involves everything from identifying, attracting, screening, shortlisting, interviewing, selecting, hiring, and onboarding employees. The recruitment teams can be large or small depending on the size of an organization. However, in smaller organizations, recruitment is typically the responsibility of a recruiting manager. Many companies of today, use recruitment software to make their recruitment process more effective and efficient. The recruitment process is a process of identifying the job vacancy, analysing the job requirements, reviewing applications, screening, shortlisting and selecting the right candidate.

1. Recruitment Planning:

The first step involved in the recruitment process is planning. Here, planning involves drafting a comprehensive job specification for the vacant position, outlining its major and minor responsibilities; the skills, experience and qualifications needed; grade and level of pay; starting date;

whether temporary or permanent; and mention of special conditions, if any, attached to the job to be filled "

2. Strategy Development:

Once it is known how many with what qualifications of candidates are required, the next step involved in this regard is to devise a suitable strategy for recruiting the candidates in the organisation

3. Searching:

This step involves attracting job seekers to the organisation. There are broadly two sources used to attract candidates

Internal and External Sources

4. Screening:

Though some view screening as the starting point of selection, we have considered it as an integral part of recruitment. The reason being the selection process starts only after the applications have been screened and shortlisted.

5. Evaluation and Control:

Given the considerable cost involved in the recruitment process, its evaluation and control is, therefore, imperative.

The costs generally incurred in a recruitment process include:

(i) Salary of recruiters

(ii) Cost of time spent for preparing job analysis, advertisement

(iii) Administrative expenses

(iv) Cost of outsourcing or overtime while vacancies remain unfilled

SOURCES OF RECRUITMENT

Whenever there is a vacancy in the organization, generally it is to be filled. To make the candidate available for filling those vacancies, their selection procedure and placement on a proper job comes under the purview of recruitment.

As soon as the available vacancies are known, they are advertised through different media and accordingly the applications are collected for the vacant posts. A group of candidates interested in doing the job and are eligible to do, it is created through recruitment.

Internal Sources of Recruitment:

1. Promotions:

Promotion results in enhancements in pay, position, responsibility and authority. The important requirement for implementation of the promotion policy is that the terms, conditions, rules and regulations should be well-defined.

2. Retirements:

The retired employees may be given the extension in their service in case of non-availability of suitable candidates for the post.

3. Former employees:

Former employees who had performed well during their tenure may be called back, and higher wages and incentives can be paid to them.

4. Transfer:

Employees may be transferred from one department to another wherever the post becomes vacant.

External Sources of Recruitment:

1. Press advertisement:

A wide choice for selecting the appropriate candidate for the post is available through this source. It gives publicity to the vacant posts and the details about the job in the form of job description and job specification are made available to public in general.

2. Campus interviews:

It is the best possible method for companies to select students from various educational institutions. It is easy and economical. The company officials personally visit various institutes and select students eligible for a particular post through interviews.

3. Placement agencies:

A databank of candidates is sent to organizations for their selection purpose and agencies get commission in return.

4. Employment exchange:

People register themselves with government employment exchanges with their personal details. According to the needs and request of the organization, the candidates are sent for interviews.

5. Walk in interviews:

These interviews are declared by companies on the specific day and time and conducted for selection.

METHODS OF RECRUITMRNET

1. Hire for Attitude and Train for Skills

A valuable employee is one with the right attitude for your organization. By attitude we are referring to a person's thought, manner, and general disposition towards another person, idea, activity, object, or thing. Their attitude will be reflected in their behaviour, which can either be positive or negative.

2. Thinking outside the Box

Recruiters are starting to redefine the hiring process and the future thinkers are now beginning to really question the actual usefulness of the resume. How can two pages where candidates simply list their skills and experience really tell us about the candidate's fit and attitude?

3. Go Where They Go

If you want to get in touch with your ideal candidates, then you should go where they go, do what they do, and read what they read. To find your ideal chef, read up on their industry, use professional magazines or publications, and visit industry events.

4. Employee Referral Programs

An organization's current employees are great sources of knowledge for recruitment. Employees will most likely have friends or acquaintances that are in the same field. Employee referral programs can therefore be effective means for recruitment

5. Databases

Recruiters collect and retain applications from all past job postings. Even if a candidate wasn't chosen for a given position, chances are they will still have their details on file thanks to CRM software.

Q2 Explain steps involved in selection

Finding the interested candidates who have submitted their profiles for a particular job is the process of recruitment, and choosing the best and most suitable candidates among them is the process of selection. Selection process narrows down the scope and becomes specific when it selects the suitable candidates.

According to Harold Koontz, "Selection is the process of choosing from the candidates, from within the organization or from outside, the most suitable person for the current position or for the future positions."

Steps Involved in Selection Procedure:

The selection procedure followed by different organizations, many times, becomes lengthy as it is a question of getting the most suitable candidates for which various tests are to be done and interviews to be taken.

1. Inviting applications:

The prospective candidates from within the organization or outside the organization are called for applying for the post.

2. Receiving applications:

Detailed applications are collected from the candidates which provide the necessary information about personal and professional details of a person. These applications facilitate analysis and comparison of the candidates.

3. Scrutiny of applications:

As the limit of the period within which the company is supposed to receive applications ends, the applications are sorted out.

4. Written tests:

As the final list of candidates becomes ready after the scrutiny of applications, the written test is conducted. This test is conducted for understanding the technical knowledge, attitude and interest of the candidates.

5. Psychological tests:

These tests are conducted individually and they help for finding out the individual quality and skill of a person. The types of psychological tests are aptitude test, intelligence test, synthetic test and personality test

6. Personal interview:

Candidates proving themselves successful through tests are interviewed personally. The interviewers may be individual or a panel.

7. Reference check:

Generally, at least two references are asked for by the company from the candidate. Reference check is a type of crosscheck for the information provided by the candidate through their application form and during the interviews.

8. Medical examination:

Physical strength and fitness of a candidate is must before they takes up the job.

9. Final selection:

At this step, the candidate is given the appointment letter to join the organization on a particular date. The appointment letter specifies the post, title, salary and terms of employment.

10. Placement:

This is a final step. A suitable job is allocated to the appointed candidate so that they can get the whole idea about the nature of the job.

Q1 Explain need and importance of Training and development

Training and Development is one of the main functions of the human resource management department. Training refers to a systematic setup where employees are instructed and taught matters of technical knowledge related to their jobs. Whereas, Development refers to the overall holistic and educational growth and maturity of people in managerial positions,

Training and development refers to educational activities within a company created to enhance the knowledge and skills of employees while providing information and instruction on how to better perform specific tasks.

According to Garry Dessler, "Training is the process of teaching new employees the basic skills they need to perform their jobs."

Training is a social and continuous process of increasing the skills, knowledge, attitudes, and efficiency of employees for getting better performance in the organization.

Benefits of training and development

- Employee training and development increases job satisfaction and morale among employees.
- Reduces employee turnover.
- Increases employee motivation.
- Increases efficiencies in processes, resulting in financial gain.

Need for Training

Every organization should provide training to all the employees irrespective of their qualifications and skills.

Specifically the need for training arises because of following reasons:

1. Environmental changes:

Mechanization, computerization, and automation have resulted in many changes that require trained staff possessing enough skills

2. Organizational complexity:

With modern inventions, technological upgradation, and diversification most of the organizations have become very complex. This has aggravated the problems of coordination. So, in order to cope up with the complexities, training has become mandatory.

Training of Employees - Need and Importance of
Training — HotellerieJobs

3. Human relations:

Every management has to maintain very good human relations, and this has made training as one of the basic conditions to deal with human problems.

4. Change in the job assignment:

Training is also necessary when the existing employee is promoted to the higher level or transferred to another department. Training is also required to equip the old employees with new techniques and technologies.

Importance of Training:

Training and development is important for the following reasons:-

1. Creating a Highly Skilled, Motivated and Enthusiastic Workforce
2. Increase Productivity
3. To Improve Quality of Work
4. To Decrease Learning Period
5. Build Team Spirit
6. Healthy Work Environment
7. To Reduce Cost
8. To Improve Health and Safety
9. To Improve Organisational Climate
10. Personal Growth of Employees
11. Improve Employee Morale
12. Better Managerial Skills
13. Skill Enhancement
14. Reduce Employee Turnover.

Q2. Explain different types of training with process of designing a training program.

A small business may offer training in information technology for its workforce. A large corporation may have compulsory on boarding activities for employees joining for the first time. Implementing training for unique companies differs in many aspects

The best types of employee training methods for your workforce may include:

1. **Instructor-led training**

Instructor-led training is the traditional type of employee training that occurs in a classroom, with a teacher presenting the material. This can be a highly effective method of employee training, especially for complex topics.

2. **ELearning**

ELearning, on the other hand, relies on online videos, tests, and courses to deliver employee training. Employees can do their training right in the palm of their hand with a smartphone or on their company computers.

3. Simulation employee training

Simulation training is most often provided through a computer, argumented, or virtual reality device. Despite the initial costs for producing that software or technology, however, simulation training can be a necessary option for employees in riskier or high-stakes fields

4. Hands-on training

Hands-on training includes any experiential training that's focused on the individual needs of the employee. It's conducted directly on the job.

5. Coaching or mentoring

Coaching or mentoring can share similar qualities to hands-on training, but in this type of employee training, the focus is on the relationship between an employee and a more experienced professional, such as their supervisor, a coach, or a veteran employee.

6. Lecture-style training

Important for getting big chunks of information to a large employee population, lecture-style training can be an invaluable resource for communicating required information quickly.

7. Group discussions and activities

For the right group of employees, group discussions and activities can provide the perfect training option. It allows multiple employees to train at once, in an environment that better fits their current departments or groups.

8. Role-playing

Similar to group discussions, role-playing specifically asks employees to work through one aspect of their jobs in a controlled scenario. They'll be asked to consider different points-of-view and think on their feet as they work through the role-playing activity.

9. Management-specific activities

Management-specific activities are just that—employee training that's focused on the needs of managers. They may include simulations, brainstorming activities, team-building exercises, role-playing, or focused eLearning on management best practices.

10. Case studies or other required reading

Finally, some employee training topics are readily accessible through required readings. Case studies, in particular, can provide a quick way for employees to learn about real workplace issues.

PROCESS OF DESIGNING A TRAINING PROGRAM

The training program is defined as an activity or activities that include undertaking one or a series of courses to boost performance, productivity, skills, and knowledge.

Many problems occur in the process of designing a training program. Some of the common problems are; creating training that does not support a business goal, problems that training cannot fix, how to identify the purpose of a training program

Below are the five steps that show how to create a more effective training program:

Step 1: Perform a Training Needs Assessment

- Identifying the business goal that can be supported by a training program.
- Determining the tasks that workers should perform to make the company reach its goals.
- Conducting the training activities that will help in enhancing the learning of the workers to perform the tasks more effectively.
- Determining the learning characteristics of the workers that will make the training effective.

Step 2: Develop Learning Objectives

- What is the product flow?
- How to maintain the product flow cycle?
- Importance of good product lifecycle.

Step 3: Design Training Materials

- Focus on the learning needs of your employees.
- Create training assessments that can directly relate to the learning objectives.
- Remember the adult learning philosophies.
- Include more hands-on practice or simulation as possible.

Step 4: Implement the Training

Implementation can take different forms by moving forward to the training. It can be classroom instructions, the completion of e-learning modules, or more.

Step 5: Evaluate the Training

- Employees' reaction to training.
- Employees' learning through the training.
- Employee's job behaviour post-training.
- Beneficial business results.

Explain Training Evaluation

Training evaluation is the systematic process of analysing if training programs and initiatives are effective and efficient. The evaluation process is beneficial as it can assess the usefulness of the process, help in overall working and boost employee engagement. Training evaluation refers to the process of collecting the outcomes needed to determine if training is effective. The company constantly evaluates the effectiveness of training programs to find if the money they have invested has been spending properly or not.

Benefits

Evaluation of training gives comprehensive feedback on the value of the training programs and their effectiveness in achieving business goals.

It also helps the organization to:

- Identify issues and improve the overall processes of training programs;

- Analyse the effectiveness of training materials and other tools;
- Determine the needed leadership competencies to solve critical problems;
- Support continuous change in career development; and
- Assess the overall training experience of the participants

Training programs can be evaluated by asking the following questions.

1. Has change occurred after training?
2. Is the change due to training?
3. Is the change positive or negative?
4. Will the change continue with every training program?

The different types of training evaluation program are-

Formative evaluation – This type of training evaluation offers feedback to the developer and designer of the program.

Process evaluation– This type of training evaluation deals in information related to events occurred during training.

Outcome evaluation – This type of training evaluation determines whether results were achieved after applying new skills and know-how.

Impact evaluation – This type of training evaluation deals with the impact of the training on the strategic goals of a company.

Training evaluation methods

Evaluation methods are conducted to know where the objectives were met and the impact of training on performance levels. There are two types of training evaluation methods

Qualitative method

- Focus groups
- Case studies
- Interviews

The quantitative method

- Experiments
- Surveys

4 Steps of Evaluation Process of Training Program

These 4 questions give the 4 steps of evaluating training Program:-

1. Reaction
2. Learning
3. Behaviour
4. Result

1. Reaction
Reaction refers to the attitude of employees about the training, whether the employee considers training to be a positive or negative one

2. Learning
Another method of judging effectiveness is to identify levels of learning i.e., how much the people have learned during the training

3. Behaviour
The HR department needs to understand the behaviour of the employees, to understand the effectiveness of training.

4. Result
Results provided by the employee in monetary terms also determine the effectiveness of the training program, i.e., employee success in handling the project, the group performance before and after training, etc.

what is Executive Development?
Executive development is a process of bringing **change in behaviour, performance and adaptability.** It helps in gaining skills, knowledge, and growth to become a better leader. The purpose of executive development in hrm is to develop an attitude of adaptability to new and tough situations. So, it will improve their *decision and problem-solving skills.*

Objectives of Executive Development

1. Sustain in a dynamic and competitive environment
2. Ensure competent staff at all levels
3. Develop leaders
4. Executive Career Growth

Characteristic of Executive Development:

- Development is a planned and organized process of learning rather than a haphazard or trial and error approach.
- It is an ongoing or never ending exercise rather than a 'one shot' affair.

- Executive development is a long term process as managerial skills cannot be developed over night.
- Executive Development is guided self-development. An organisation can provide opportunities for development of its present and potential managers.

What is career development?

Career development is the series of activities or the on-going/lifelong process of developing one's career which includes defining new goals regularly and acquiring skills to achieve them. Career development is the process of managing life, learning and work over the lifespan

According to Edwin Flippo, "A career is sequence of separate but related work activities that provide continuity, order and meaning to a person's life."

Career development is essential for implementation of career plan. While career plan sets career path for an employee, career development ensures that the employee is well developed before he moves up the next higher ladder in the hierarchy.

IMPORTANCE OF CAREER DEVELOPMENT

The main objective of career development is to ensure that people with appropriate qualifications and experiences are available when needed.

The focus of career development is on the following:

(i) Obtaining relevant information about individual employees' interests and preferences;

(ii) Matching individuals' career interests and aptitudes to job requirements;

(iii) Providing career path information to employees to enable them to make their career plans;

(iv) Providing financial inducements and facilities to employees for acquisition of new skills and capabilities

5 Steps of Career Development

There are various steps or stages in a person's overall career development:

1. Self-Assessment

The first step in career development is the self-assessment which means that the individual has to assess oneself on the kind of career and growth one wants and what kind of skills and interests are there.

2. Career Awareness

This stage is when an individual explores various career paths which align with the self-assessment done in the first step.

3. Goal Setting

This is the most important step in career development because this is where one defines clear short term and long term goals to meet the career one aspires.

4. Skill Training

Once the career and goals are set, one needs to acquire the right skills to achieve the growth. Skill training can be done through self-training or joining a structured training program online or offline

5. Performing

With all the right knowledge and skills, the important part is to perform the tasks and jobs in the career successfully to grow in the career path.

The 5 steps are part of an ongoing process. Many times in a career, the person would need to revisit the cycle to get the right career growth.

THREE

JOB EVALUATION, WAGE DETERMINATION, FRINGE BENEFITS,EXECUTIVE COMPENSATION & PERFORMANCE APPRAISAL

Introduction

Job Evaluation

The **Job Evaluation** is the process of assessing the relative worth of the jobs in an organization. The jobs are evaluated on the basis of its content and the complexity involved in its operations and thus, positioned according to its importance. Job evaluation is the systematic process of determining the relative value of different jobs in an organization. The goal of job evaluation is to compare jobs with each other in order to create a pay structure that is fair, equitable, and consistent for everyone.

In the words of **Dale Yoder,** *"Job evaluation is a practice which seeks to provide a degree of objectivity in measuring the comparative value of jobs within an organisation and among similar organisations."*

This ensures that everyone is paid their worth and that different jobs have different entry and performance requirements.

The objectives of job evaluation

- To establish an orderly, rational, systematic structure of jobs based on their worth to the organization.
- To justify an existing pay rate structure or to develop one that provides for internal equity.
- To assist in setting pay rates that are comparable to those of in similar jobs in other organizations to compete in market place for best talent.
- To provide a rational basis for negotiating pay rates when bargaining collectively with a recognized union.
- To ensure the fair and equitable compensation of employees in relation to their duties.

Job Evaluation Methods

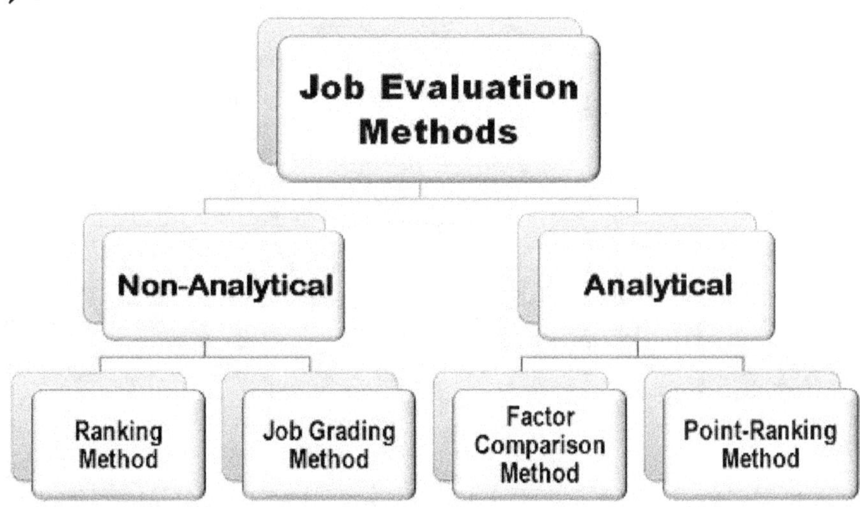

Non-analytical Job Evaluation Methods

- **Ranking Method**: This is the simplest and inexpensive job evaluation method, wherein the jobs are ranked from the highest to the lowest on the basis of their importance in the organization. In this method, the overall job is compared with the other set of jobs and then is given a rank on the basis of its content and complexity in performing it.
- **Job Grading Method**: Also known as **Job-Classification Method.** Under this method, the job grades or classes are predetermined and then each job is assigned to these and is evaluated accordingly.

Analytical Job Evaluation Methods

- **Factor-Comparison Method**: Under this method, the job is evaluated, and the ranks are given on the basis of a series of factors Viz. Mental effort, physical effort, skills required for supervisory responsibilities, working conditions, and other relevant factors.
- **Point-Ranking Method**: Under this method, each job's key factor is identified and then the sub-factors are determined. These sub-factors are then assigned the points by its importance.

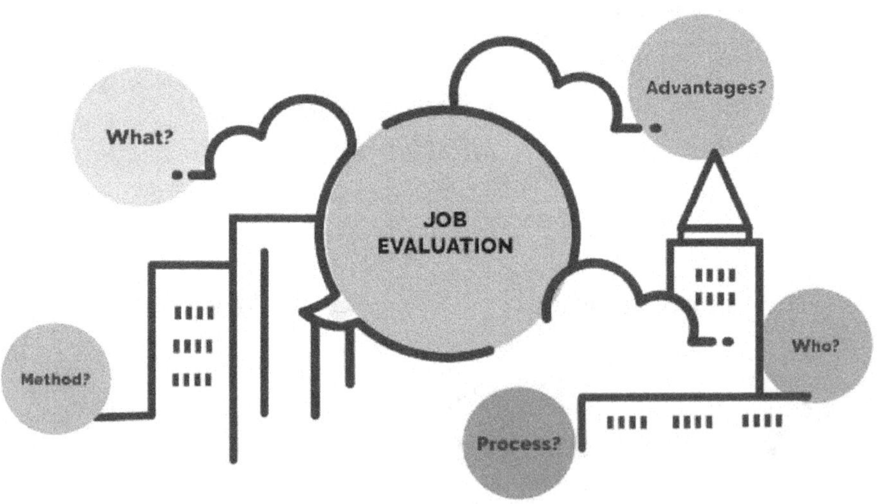

Features of Job Evaluation

- It attempts to assess jobs, not people.
- Job evaluation is the output provided by job analysis.
- Job evaluation does not design wage structure, it helps in rationalising the system by reducing number of separate and different rates.
- Job evaluation is not made by individuals rather it is done by group of experts.

Advantages of Job evaluation

- **Reduction in inequalities in salary structure**
- **Helps in selection of employees**
- **Relevance of new jobs**
- **Harmonious relationship between employees and manager**

The job evaluation process
The job evaluation process involves four steps

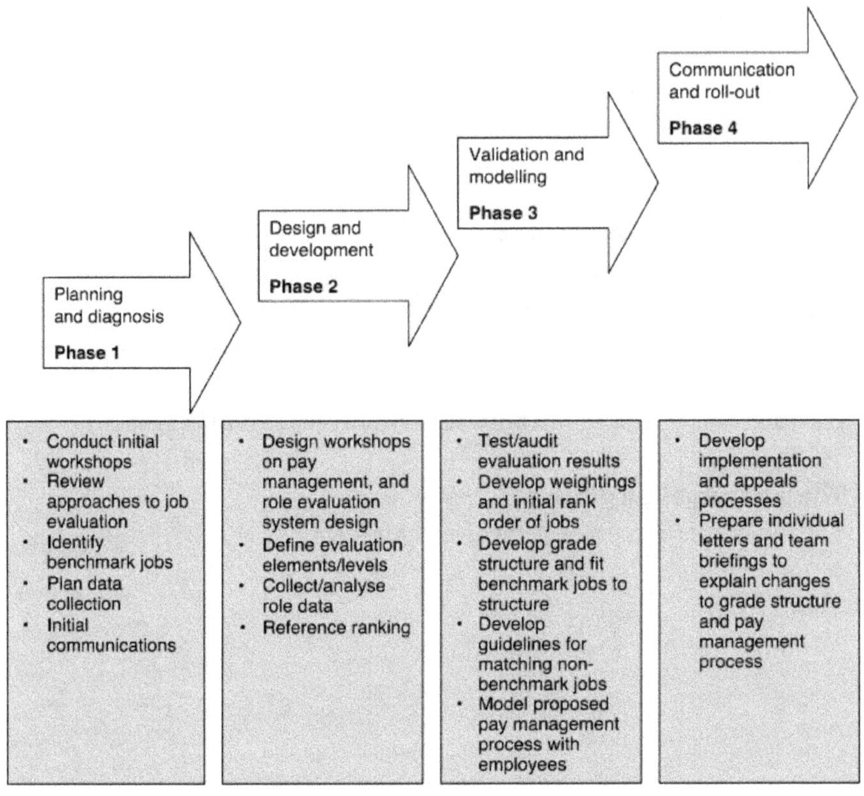

what is wage determination? What are different types of wages?

Wages are compensation for an employee's personal services, whether paid by check or cash, or the reasonable cash value of noncash payments such as meals and lodging. Payments are considered wages even if the employee is a casual worker, a day or contract labourer, part-time or temporary worker, or paid by the day, hour, or any other method or measurement.

Wages include, but are not limited to:

- Salaries, hourly pay, piece rate, or payments by the job.
- Commissions and bonuses.
- Overtime and vacation pay.
- The reasonable cash value of compensation other than cash.

"Wages is the payment to labour for its assistance to production." -A.H. Hansen

Wage Determination

The process of determining wages involves a series of interrelated steps

1. Job Analysis: It involves the identification and precisely identifying the required tasks, the knowledge and skills necessary for performing them and the conditions under which they must be performed.

2. Job Evaluation: It is the formal process used to assign wage and salary rates to job. A variety of systems and products exist to guide this process, each different from the other in packaging, pricing, philosophy, procedures and utility.

3. Conduct the Salary Survey: Once the process of job evaluation has determined the relative worth of jobs, the actual amounts to be paid must be determined. This is done by making wage or salary surveys in the area concerned.

4. Grouping of Similar Jobs into Similar Grades – Pay Grades: Once the relative worth of each job is determined, the task of assigning pay rate to each job is done which is possible only by first grouping jobs into pay grades

5. Preparation of Wage Structure – Wage Curves: The next step is to determine the wage structure

6. Developing Pay Ranges – (Wage Structure): It is only a short step from plotting a wage curve to developing the organization wage structure. Jobs that are similar in terms of classes, grades or points are grouped together.

7. Wage Administration Rules: Once the pay ranges have been determined, the development of rules of wage administration has to be done.

Types of Wages:

Piece Wages: Piece wages are the wages paid according to the work done by the worker. To calculate the piece wages, the number of units produced by the worker are taken into consideration.

Time Wages: If the labourer is paid for his services according to time, it is called as time wages. For example, if the labour is paid Rs. 35 per day, it will be termed as time wage.

Cash Wages: Cash wages refer to the wages paid to the labour in terms of money. The salary paid to a worker is an instance of cash wages.

Wages in Kind: When the labourer is paid in terms of goods rather than cash, is called the wage in kind. These types of wages are popular in rural areas.

Contract Wages: Under this type, the wages are fixed in the beginning for complete work. For instance, if a contractor is told that he will be paid Rs. 25,000 for the construction of building, it will be termed as contract wages.

Explain salary structure

Salary structure is a compensation structure is the strategy you use to determine how each employee in your company is paid. It considers information like the length of employment, industry minimums and maximums, and merit. Salary structures are an important component of effective compensation programs and help ensure that pay levels for groups of jobs are competitive externally and equitable internally. A well-designed salary structure allows management to reward performance and skills development while controlling overall base salary cost by providing a cap on the range paid for particular jobs or locations

Wage structure is the hierarchy within a company that sets the amount each level of employment is paid and what benefits each level is due. Lower-level employees are paid less than other people at the business, and these employees may get an hourly wage as opposed to a set salary.

Common Compensation Structures

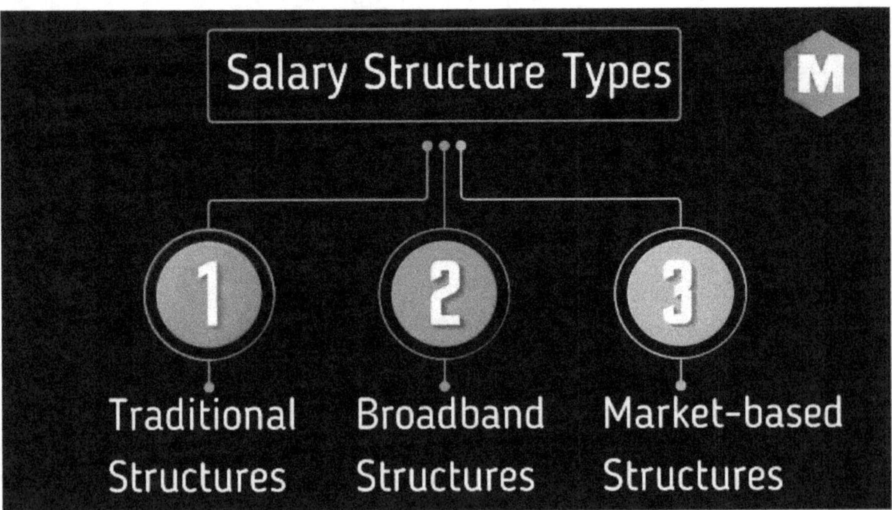

Traditional Structure

In this compensation category, numerous pay grades are assigned per position. As an employee moves up based on performance, merit, or time at the position, they move up to the next pay grade.

Market-Based Structure

A market-based structure is exactly what it sounds like. By researching market data based on what other employers are paying for similar job positions, you can determine what you should pay. This structure still uses pay grades, and it can be set at a minimum that's on par with what your competitors pay.

Broadband Structure

In this lesser-used compensation plan, there are fewer pay grades and the overall salary ranges are bigger. There is more flexibility to give raises within the same pay grade without also moving an employee up one level.

What are fringe benefits?

Fringe benefits are additions to compensation that companies give their employees. Some fringe benefits are given universally to all employees of a company while others may be offered only to those at executive levels. Some benefits are awarded to compensate employees for costs related to their work while others are geared to general job satisfaction.

The term fringe benefits refers to the extra benefits provided to employees in addition to the normal compensation paid in the form of wage or salary.

The National Industrial Conference Board (U.S.A.) has defined "fringe benefits" as "payments to workers over and above the wages paid on the basis of time worked or production completed."

Fringe benefits include status (cars, entertainment facilities, holidays, foreign travel, telephone); security (insurance, medical facilities, children's education), and work benefits (office accommodation, secretarial services, management training, company scholarships etc.).

Examples of fringe benefits:

(A) Statutory benefits – The Employees Provident Fund Scheme, Gratuity or Pension Schemes and Employees State Insurance Scheme.

(B) Non-statutory benefits – Payments towards Employees Provident Fund Scheme, Gratuity and Pension Fund contribution, medical facilities, canteens, uniform and recreational facilities.

Features of fringe benefits:

(A) They are paid to all employees (unlike incentives which are paid to specific employees whose work is above standard) based on their membership in the organization.

(B) They are supplementary forms of compensation.

(C) They help raise the living conditions of employees.

(D) They are indirect compensation because they are usually extended as a condition of employment and are not directly related to performance.

The fringe benefits are classified as:

Employment Security: Benefits under this head include unemployment, insurance, technological adjustment pay, leave travel pay, overtime pay, level for negotiation, leave for maternity, leave for grievances, holidays, cost of living bonus, call-back pay, lay-off, retiring rooms, jobs to the sons/ daughters of the employees and the like.

Health Protection: Benefits under this head include accident insurance, disability insurance, health insurance, hospitalization, life insurance, medical care, sick benefits, sick leave, etc.

Old Age and Retirement: Benefits under this category include deferred income plans, pension, gratuity, provident fund, old age assistance, old age counselling, and medical benefits for retired employees, traveling concession to retired employees, jobs to sons/daughters of the deceased employee and the like.

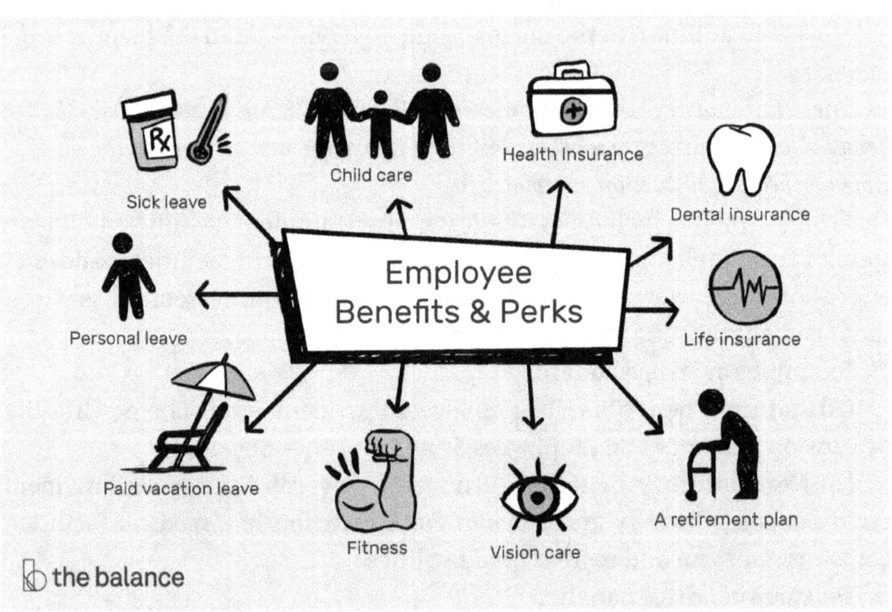

Personnel Identification, Participation and Stimulation: This category covers the benefits like anniversary awards, attendance bonus, canteen, cooperative credit societies, educational facilities, beauty parlour services, housing, income tax aid, counselling, quality bonus, recreational programs, stress counselling, safety measures, etc.

Extra Pay for Time Worked: This category covers the benefits such as premium pay, incentive bonus, shift premium, old age insurance, profit sharing, unemployment compensation, Christmas bonus, Diwali or Pooja bonus, food cost subsidy, housing subsidy, recreation.

Payment for Time Not Worked: Benefits under this category include sick leave with pay, vacation pay, paid rest and relief time, paid lunch periods, grievance time, bargaining time, travel time, etc.

What is executive compensation?

Executive compensation is the monetary and non-monetary benefits which are given to the senior management & executives of a company. Executive compensation includes salaries, perks, incentives, insurances etc.

This includes high salaries for executive, insurances, company shares & other benefits.

The **Executive Compensation**refers to the financial payment and other non-monetary rewards given to the top executives in exchange for their services to the organization.

The kind of employees that are entitled to the executive compensation are corporate presidents, vice-presidents, chief executive officers, chief financial officers and other senior executives.

Importance of executive compensation

It is an important aspect of business and HRM. Senior employees are the ones making the strategies, taking importance decisions etc. Thus, it is extremely important to keep the senior management motivated. The Executive compensation is negotiable between the employer and potential executive. It can defy the organizational norms on compensation to regular employees. Executive compensation is offered to the chairman, CEOs, board of directors etc.

Components of executive compensation

The various components of executive compensation are –

1. Salary – base salary
2. Short Term Incentives (STI) – for meeting the short term goals
3. Long Term Incentives (LTI) – There are the incentives which are paid after a period more than a year (usually 3-5 years) like offering restricted stocks
4. Guaranteed Severance Package
5. Perquisites – like club memberships, private planes,
6. Insurance – health insurance for self and dependents

What are the needs and importance of performance appraisal?

A performance appraisal is a part of measuring, comparing, finding, guiding, correcting and managing career development of the employees. It is the process of gathering, recording and critically analysing information about the relative importance of employees to the organisation.

"It is the evaluation or appraisal of the relative worth to the company of a man's services on his job." (Alford and Beatty)

Performance appraisal is study of present achievements and failures, personal strengths and weaknesses, and suitability for incentives, rewards and recognition, increased pay scale, promotion or further training.

Purpose of Performance Appraisal

1. To provide employees with the feedback on their performance for further improvement.
2. To categorize the employees as high, moderate and low performers.
3. To identify the need for employee training.
4. To plan for future requirements of human resources.

Need For Performance Appraisal:

1. Evaluation of an employee's performance helps to take management decisions on transfers, promotions, increments etc.
2. Performance appraisal helps to ascertain the training and development needs of the employer.
3. Performance appraisal. or an individual's performance evaluation helps in designing the reward system.
4. The feedback presided after evaluating the performance of an individual acts as a motivator.
5. The Performance appraisal acts as a validation of the selection procedure.

Features of Performance Appraisal:

1. It is the systematic description of an employee's job relevant strengths and weaknesses.
2. Finding how well the employee is performing the job and establishing a plan of improvement is the basic purpose.
3. Performance appraisal is periodical.
4. Performance appraisal is not job evaluation, but finding how well someone is doing the assignable job.

Importance of Performance Appraisal

Assessment of Employee Performance: Performance appraisal helps supervisors to assess the work performance of their subordinates

Improvement of Performance: The performance of employees are continuously scanned and reviewed. This creates a psychological pressure on employees to perform well, as well as motivates the employees

Designing Training and Development Programme: Training and development programme are designed considering the existing skill, knowledge, capability and performance of the employees as disclosed by performance appraisal.

Determination of Pay: Bonus and increment of salary is determined on the basis of performance of employees.

Decision Regarding Promotion and Transfer: Performance appraisal on a continuous basis helps to evaluate the improvement of employee performance, their skill, knowledge, capability so that they can be allotted a new job.

Explain the process of performance appraisal

Performance appraisal is a systematic evaluation of the employee's present job capabilities and also his potential for growth and development by his superiors. It can be either informal or formal.

The performance appraisal process has been used as a deciding factor for career development, and in most cases, the promotions and salary raise are directly dependent on it.

The performance appraisal process should be calculated over some time so that both the employer and employee can have a better idea about his performance on an annual basis.

The appraisal process consists of six steps

Step 1: Establish performance standards

Standards are based on the position, rather than an individual. In order to be clearly understood and perceived as objective, standards should adhere to the same rules that apply to goal-setting

Step 2: Communicate performance standards

In order to be effective, performance standards must be clearly communicated and understood to be expectations. Performance standards assume that an individual is competent, so initial and corrective training should be factored into the performance management process.

Step 3: Measure performance

Performance that is expressed in numeric terms—for example, cost, quantity, quality, timeliness—is relatively easy to measure. Performance in the area of soft skills—for example, communication, customer service and leadership—is more difficult to evaluate. The focus should be on measuring what matters rather than measuring what's easy to measure.

Step 4: Compare actual performance to performance standards

In this step of the appraisal process, actual performance is compared to the performance standards. Documentation should highlight actions and results.

Step 5: Discuss the appraisal with the employee

This is generally the step in the process that is the most difficult for managers and employees alike and it can be a challenge to manage emotions and expectations. Even when performance is strong, there can be differences of opinion on the next action. A significant difference of opinion regarding performance can create an emotionally-charged situation.

Step 6: Implement personnel action

The final step in the appraisal process is the discussion and/or implementation of any next steps: a reward of some sort—a raise, promotion or coveted development opportunity—or corrective action—a performance plan or termination.

What are the methods of performance appraisal?

Each method of performance appraisal has its strengths and weaknesses may be suitable for one organisation and non-suitable for another one. As such, there is no single appraisal method accepted and used by all organisations to measure their employees' performance.

A more widely used classification of appraisal methods into two categories, viz., traditional methods and modem methods, is given by Strauss and Sayles". While traditional methods lay emphasis on the rating of the individual's personality traits, such as initiative, dependability, drive creativity, integrity, intelligence, leadership potential, etc.; the modem methods, on the other hand, place more emphasis on the evaluation of work results, i.e., job achievements than the personal traits!

Methods Of Performance Appraisal

- **Past-oriented Methods** (Also known as Traditional Methods of Performance Appraisal)

  1. Rating Scales
  2. Checklists
  3. Forced Choice
  4. Forced Distribution
  5. Critical Incident
  6. Performance test and observation
  7. Field review
  8. Confidential Record
  9. Essay method
  10. Comparative Evaluation Approaches
  11. Cost Accounting Method

12.   Behaviourally Anchored Rating Scales

- **Future Oriented Methods** (Also known asModern Methods of Performance Appraisal)

1.   Management by objectives
2.   Psychological Appraisal
3.   Assessment Centres
4.   360-Degree Feedback
5.   720-Degree Feedback

Different types of performance appraisal methods

1. Straight ranking appraisals: This compares all employees to each other, ranking them from best to worst. Whilst it may be easy to see who's a high flier and who's not making the cut, everyone in the middle will be harder to rank.

2. Grading: This systematic method that allows a manager to quickly see an employee's level for any given skill e.g. teamwork, communication, attention to detail etc. They could be scored A – F or 1 – 5 or even from unacceptable through to excellent. This method is also subjective and so could be seen as unreliable if used alone.

3. Management by objective: The thinking behind this modern method is based around both employee and manager jointly setting goals to be achieved within a specific time period. This form of appraisal is a process rather than a one-off evaluation and it's all about planning and being proactive rather than reactive to events and circumstances.

4. Trait and behaviour-based appraisals: Trait-based appraisals assess characteristics that contribute to an individual's personality, such as creativity, extroversion and confidence. This might be how warmly a customer service advisor speaks to a customer, for example.

5. 360-degree appraisals: This method involves feedback from several people who have contact with each employee, keeping biases firmly at bay. This could be several other colleagues, clients, customers etc. and even the employee themselves is required to offer their view of their role in the team. 360-degree appraisal is hailed as the best approach because it's all-encompassing (the secrets in the name!) and can give such a well-rounded view of an employee.

Importance Of Performance Appraisal

Performance appraisals give crucial and helpful data for evaluating an employee's skill, knowledge, ability, and overall job performance. The following are some of the reasons why performance appraisal is so important in an organisation:

1. Employee skill, knowledge, ability, and overall job performance are all assessed via performance appraisals. The following are some examples of why performance appraisal is so important in a company:

2. Employee training and development needs can be accessed via performance appraisal.

3. Employees can use performance appraisal to remedy their faults, as well as receive adequate guidance and criticism for their progress.

4. Better performance is rewarded with a performance appraisal.

5. The improvement of the organization's communication system is aided by performance appraisal.

6. The effectiveness of human resource programmes implemented in the organisation is evaluated through performance appraisal.

7. The preparation of a pay structure for each person working in the firm is aided by performance appraisal.

8. Employee potential is assessed through performance appraisal, and future capability is forecasted.

Performance Appraisal Process

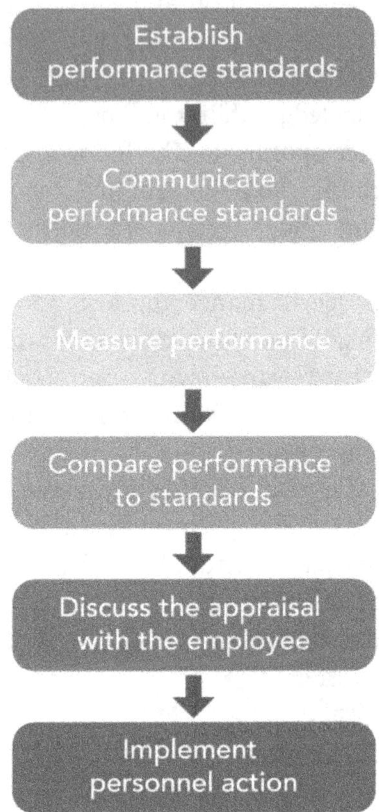

Source: courses.lumenlearning.com

◦ **Step 1: Establish performance standards**

Performance standards are established to guarantee that departmental goals and objectives are met, as well as the organization's overarching strategy and goals. Individuals are not held to the same standards as positions. Standards should follow the same rules as goals in order to be readily understood and viewed as objective; that is, they should be "SMART:" precise, measurable, achievable, relevant, and timebound.

◦ **Step 2: Communicate performance standards**

Performance standards must be properly communicated and acknowledged to be expectations in order to be effective. Initial and corrective training should be integrated into the performance management process since performance criteria presuppose that an employee is competent. It should also be disclosed whether there is a defined training period after which an employee is regarded to be competent and performing to standards.

◦ **Step 3: Measure performance**

Cost, quantity, quality, and timeliness are examples of quantitative performance that is relatively easy to quantify. Soft skills performance, including as communication, customer service, and leadership, is more difficult to assess. Personal observation, oral reporting, and written reports are among the sources of knowledge recommended by DiCenzo, Robbins, and Verhulst. They do point out, however, that what is measured is likely more important than how it is measured. [2] Instead than assessing what is easy to measure, the focus should be on measuring what matters.

◦ **Step 4: Compare actual performance to performance standards**

Actual performance is compared against performance standards in this step of the appraisal process. Actions and outcomes should be highlighted in documentation.

◦ **Step 5: Discuss the appraisal with the employee**

This is usually the most challenging part in the process for both managers and employees, and it can be tough to manage emotions and expectations. Even when performance is excellent, there may be disagreements about the next course of action. An emotionally charged scenario might arise when there is a major difference of opinion over performance. This shouldn't be the case if the boss is regularly providing feedback and coaching. A related point: If an employee's performance is continuously bad, the problem should be addressed immediately, with corrective action implemented, rather than being deferred to an annual review. Management can ask employees to complete and submit a self-evaluation prior to the appraisal meeting to identify and prepare for differences of opinion. The manager's ability to remain cool and respectful will have a tremendous impact on the employee's confidence, motivation, and future performance.

- **Step 6: Implement personnel action**

The discussion and/or implementation of any next steps: a reward of some sort—a raise, promotion, or sought growth opportunity—or corrective action—a performance plan or termination—is the final phase in the assessment process. Corrective action that might assist an employee meet expectations, on the other hand, should not be deferred until the next formal appraisal.

When performance gaps are detected, supervisors and managers should take the time to figure out why the employee's performance isn't meeting expectations and whether extra training and/or coaching can help the person reach those standards. As previously stated, if performance is such that termination is necessary, that action should be conducted as soon as possible.

FOUR

EMPLOYEE RELATIONSHIP MANAGEMENT

Introduction

Employee Relationship Management

Management is nothing but a technique that brings people together on a common platform and guides them so that they achieve their desired targets without fighting with each other.

Employee relationship management refers to managing the relationship between the various employees in an organization. Employee relationship management is an art that effectively monitors and manages the relation between individuals either of the same team or from different teams.

Having good employee relations is vital for a successful business plan in today's date.

It won't be wrong to say that the mantra to keep your business on track is having good mutual understanding and sharing a strong bond with the employees. Your employees are responsible for everything that happens in the workplace.

Employee relations is a term used to describe relations between employers and employees.

Employee relationship management happens when an employer manages the relation between all employees in the company. It covers the entire employee journey - it starts from an employee's first day and lasts until they leave the company.

IMPORTANCE of GOOD RELATION MANAGEMENT

1. **Heightened Employee Loyalty-** Employees don't leave their jobs. They leave their bosses.
2. **Increased Motivation-** Healthy workplace relations motivate employees to give their best and work harder.
3. **Fewer Chances of Workplace Conflicts-** allows employers to make unbiased decisions involving their workforce and mitigate any conflict within the organization.
4. **Improves the Trust and Confidence-** Great employee relations sow the seed of trust and confidence in the workplace.
5. **Ensures a Better Workplace Culture-** Employees and job seekers always desire to work for organizations with thriving work culture.
6. **Enhanced Work-life Balance-** Work-life balance is now the buzzword of every employer and employee.

7. **Better Employee Engagement**- when employees can share their views openly, employers can take proper steps to ensure better engagement.

What are different employee relationship management tools?

The responsibilities of an employee relations specialist include everything from determining whether the company's performance management system is appropriate for the workplace size and employee occupations to planning an employee recognition banquet. Specialized tools allow the employee relations specialists to stay up to date on the latest staff viewpoints and workforce trends.

DIFFERENT TOOLS ARE:

1. **Employee Opinion Surveys**- These surveys have two functions: They measure the workplace climate in terms of employee satisfaction and they serve as a tool to create action plans for managers in modifying work conditions to improve overall job satisfaction. Questions examine employee opinion in specific areas such as compensation and benefits; general employee opinion survey questions ask for feedback from employees on a variety of workplace issues, such as leadership, performance, pay and overall work attitudes.

2. **Training Aids**- The benefits of leadership training are improved relationships between supervisors and their employees as well as more effective workforce management skills. When employee relations specialists are called on to help improve supervisor and manager performance, they general use one-on-one guidance based on their expertise supplemented by materials such as tapes and books.

3. **Legal Resources**- legal resources available for researching labour and employment laws are an oft-used employee relations tool. Legal resources include subscription-based services as well as publicly available resources such as legislative summaries and news feeds.

4. **Human Resource Information Systems**- HRIS generate employee census reports and assist employee relations specialists in analysing workforce trends, compensation structure, pay practices and recruitment and selection processes.

5. **Departmental Expertise**- Employee relations specialists are usually human resources generalists with a broad knowledge base. Nevertheless, despite their exceptionally broad understanding of topics such as compensation, safety, recruitment and employee development, they rely

heavily on the expertise of HR department employees who handle employee issues in these areas day in and day out.

What are the issues in employee relation management?

Every business owner wants to have a safe and secure workplace that encourages communication and has a supportive culture. Common employee relations issues crop up again and again. This holds true for small and large businesses alike. Some of them are:

1. **Conflict Management-** Conflict can happen in any environment, and the workplace is certainly no different. Disputes between employees or a direct disagreement between an employee and business owner are situations that can occur frequently. An effective way of managing conflict is vital to the continued health of your company.

2. **Hour and Wage Issues-** To avoid federal wage and hour violations and to reduce the possibility that employees will dispute their pay checks, consider self-service timekeeping software that allows them to clock in and out from their smart devices. This encourages employees to keep track of and manage their own schedules by providing an efficient way to do so.

3. **Adequate Safety in the Workplace-** It's every business owner's worst nightmare to have an injury or accident happen to one of their employees while they are on the job. Promoting safety in the workplace should be a top priority of every business owner. This should be true no matter what industry they are in. This includes making sure all proper safety equipment is used and that the right security measures are put in place.

4. **Annual Leave Disputes-** Consider leave management software that helps you create a legal and transparent leave policy that leaves no room for dispute. Provide every employee with easy access to this policy. This type of software can also help your employees talk with HR managers about leave requests and adjustments.

5. **Timekeeping and Attendance Issues-** Timekeeping and attendance issues are common, and you can eliminate many of them by utilizing employee self-service software. Allowing employees to keep track of their time and communicate about attendance issues right from their smart devices reduces the chances for conflict and provides them a handy

benefit.

References

- https://www.aihr.com/blog/job-evaluation/
- https://www.economicsdiscussion.net/wages/wages-definition-types-and-other-details/7450
- https://www.indeed.com/career-advice/pay-salary/salaries-structure
- https://www.mbaskool.com/business-concepts/human-resources-hr-terms/3030-salary-structure.html
- https://www.complianceprime.com/blog/2019/07/29/types-of-fringe-benefits/
- https://businessjargons.com/executive-compensation.html
- https://businessjargons.com/performance-appraisal.html
- jobsoid.com
- yourarticlelibrary.com
- https://www.managementstudyguide.com/employee-relationship-management.htm
- https://www.managementstudyguide.com/employee-relationship-management.htm
- https://smallbusiness.chron.com/competencies-training-development-manager-11149.htm
- Managementstudyguide.com
- Blog.smarp.com
- Blog.vantagecircle.com
- Smallbusiness.chron.com
- economicdiscussion.net
- marketing91.com
- courses.lumenlearning.com
- citrushr.com
- yourarticlelibrary.com
- mightyrecruiter.com
- comeet.com
- shrm.org
- investopedia.com
- hrmpractice.com
- economicdiscussion.net
- mbaskool.com

REFERENCES

- <u>businessjargons.com</u>
-